MW01644269

The Watch

BY CLAY HURTUBISE, R.PH

RBY CLAY HURTUBISE, R.PH

"The Watch"
A dark comedy/drama play

Cover by Mike Geneseo

First Edition
Prescott, AZ
ISBN: 978-1-936877-37-9
Contributions by Ed Williman
Edited by Gordon Hinchen

For license requests
Please email Clay Hurtubise claycrashed@proton.me.

Dedication

To my loving partner, JAG

History of the play

Back in 2008 I was at an audition. The two directors sat behind a white fold out table. On the table, in the center, was a large chronograph watch. I thought I'd be reading from a script, instead they asked me to recite a passage from a favorite play.

Seeing the watch, I adlibbed the speech that is in this play when the son talks about 'The Watch.' The directors were impressed, but it wasn't enough for me to land the part. At the time I wrote a lot for an online site, Triond, where, if your piece were popular, you could earn some pocket change. The Watch was well received, but I had to keep my day job.

Fast forward twenty-seven years. As I'm recovering from a massive stroke, sleep can be elusive. At two o'clock one morning I started thinking about The Watch; no surprise to those that know me as my brain is always going. My first thought was to expand it into a book. The more I thought about it; I could visualize the interactions amongst the cast and a play seemed more appropriate. I confess that I went to AI and asked; what are the essentials for a good play? AI set out a list of things to do, which hopefully I have achieved!

Preface

The Watch is a comedy/drama. It follows a father and his family. As a young ex-military father he becomes obsessed with acquiring a status symbol. The breaking of the status piece symbolizes the breaking of bonds within his family. The wife, a forgiving soul, is a better person than the father deserves, even when both are in the graves.

About the author

I was born and raised in Maine, which I still refer to as home. At the age of eighteen, I ventured out to Wyoming to attend pharmacy school. Before that I had never been further west than the eastern side of Vermont. It didn't take long to fall in love with the west and I found the residents of Wyoming, even the police, to be a caring lot that as long as you showed them respect, you would be rewarded with empathy and friendship.

After pharmacy school I returned east and lived in or near North Conway for some time. A car accident which resulted in a quarter size tear of my brain took me out of work for eight years. My given first name was Christopher, but he died that night of the accident and Clay was born. After the accident I had a series of odd events that happened to me including two out-of-body experiences, and I started seeing ghosts.

In 2014 I was involved in an explosion which gave me my second and I awoke on fire from head to toes. The blast scorched the inside of my lungs. It took years to fully recover, just in time to suffer a massive stroke in 2023.

Currently I live with my husband who I met twenty-eight years ago. My left side is still mostly paralyzed, and my vision is severely limited, so I write.

The Watch
A dark comedy/drama play
By Clay Hurtubise, R. Ph.

Synopsis: A story about a man's obsession with a status symbol and what he is willing to sacrifice for it. He justifies his actions without conviction. While he loves his family, his obsession rules the day.

CAST
Characters played by five actors (and the spotlight operator).

YOUNG SON (YS). An exuberant twelve-year-old boy. He is tall and thin with dark hair. As a young boy he learns that his father, whom he loves, is a bit of a scoundrel.

TEENAGE SON (TS). Wears his hair with gel spikes. He wears chino style slacks, and short sleeve brightly colored shirt with top three buttons undone. Dress shoes. (*All variations of the son can be played by the same actor. Could be played by same boy with costume change.*)

ADULT SON (AS). Is well dressed, always in suit and tie.

YOUNG MOTHER (YM). A fit female, she is on the meek side, though she is intelligent, kind hearted, and has a quick, dry humor. While she understands her husband, she has empathy almost to a fault.

<u>OLDER MOTHER (OM).</u> Dresses poorly but cleanly, seems beaten down. Bald, wears a wig that is always moving around. Still has a sense of humor.

<u>YOUNG FATHER (YF).</u> Full head of hair, little on the chunky side. It tends to be loud. He is a narcissist yet still loves his family.

<u>MIDDLE-AGED & OLDER FATHER (OF).</u> Wears cheap suits that don't fit well. (*Can be either too small or too big.*) Hair is either balding or cut military style. Grumpy.

<u>PAWN SHOP OWNER (PS).</u> Bald chubby man wears glasses that he keeps on a chain around his neck, he is constantly putting them on and off. He has a dry sense of humor. He tends to use exaggerated hand/arm movements and often shrugs his shoulders.

<u>MISCELLANEOUS WOMAN (MW).</u> She has multiple small parts and different characters. All her characters are self-confident.

STAGE

On stage right is the interior of a Pawn Shop with a sign EZ COME EZ GO Pawn Shop. The counter is shaped as in picture. A row of bare bulb lights hangs over the counter top (under the sign); illuminated only during active scenes. Before the curtain opens Red Right Hand by Nick Cave and the Bad Seeds plays mid volume.

TABLE OF CONTENTS

THE WATCH

Obsession

SETTING: *Two white Adirondack chairs towards the front of stage are empty. Young Father (YF) and Young Mother (YM) are talking. She is holding a magazine. A clothesline loaded with clothespins is in the back. A basket of clothes*

sits under it. A beach ball sits on the stage right near the front of stage. The Beatles song 'Yellow Submarine,' plays gently throughout this scene.

YF. I know there will be more opportunities, but that advancement was mine!

YM. Calm down, we are here to relax. You've been tense ever since returning from the army. Let's leave city life behind us and enjoy this beautiful summer vacation at Lake Woebegone? Why not take your son out for a swim?

YF. Oh buttercup, you know he swims better than me! I'm tired of being upstaged by everyone, and that includes idiot sergeants and twelve-year-olds.

YM. Dear, you know that's not true.

YF. Oh. Name one thing I'm better at than anyone you know.

YM. Well, you can eat more than anyone I know! (*She giggles*.)

YF. Is that the best you can do?

YM. On such short notice, yes. (*More giggles*.) Here, go sit down, I'll make my ex-army man some lemonade with orange, just like you like it. Relax with this magazine by the beach. Say, where did that beachball come from?

YF. Oh that? It must have blown out of one of those speedboats. I left it by the shore so our son can use it, and it'll be visible if they come looking for it.

YM. Oh dear, you're so thoughtful.

YF. But yes, I will go sit down! And not too much orange in the lemonade, just a hint.

YM. Of course, pumpkin, but for heaven's sake, don't go away pouting, just go away! Ha ha, I kill myself!

As YF leaves, he sees something on the ground. It's a checkbook. He opens it up and says out loud to himself:

YF. Well I'll be, she's had a secret bank account since before we met!

YF proceeds to the chairs and sits down in the stage left chair. YM walks back to the clothesline and starts hanging clothes. She is swatting for a few moments at unseen insects. She hits her own head, yells out "Ouch" then she giggles again and resumes hanging clothes. Miscellaneous Woman (MW) enters stage right. She is wearing a summer outfit with a broad brimmed straw hat, after she passes the beachball.

MW. Excuse me, sir.

YF. Yes ma'am, how may I help you?

MW. I'm Mrs. MacMillan from the next camp. I'm looking for our beach ball. Is this one yours, or did it just blow down here from our camp?

YF. That one is ours, ma'am. You can see our name on it.

YF picks up a magic marker off the arm of the chair and puts it into his shirt pocket. MW leans over and looks closer at the ball without touching it.

MW. Oh yes, I see that. Sorry to bother you.

YF. No bother at all. I understand. After all, don't all beach balls look the same?

MW. Yes, mmm hmm, I suppose they do. Have a nice day.

YF. Thank you, and likewise.

MW exits stage left. Just before she leaves, she looks back at YF and shakes her head. Young Son (YS) comes running in from stage right. He is dressed like a clown. He is wearing white high-top sneakers and a bit too short pair of baggy blue jeans. His much too big T-shirt is black. On the front of the T-

shirt is a large yellow smiley face and, on the back, divided in two lines, it reads in bold yellow letters, "YELL LOW." He is wearing an old-fashioned derby hat. He runs around both chairs twice before standing up in the empty chair.

YS. Hi, father. Whatcha doing?

YF. Eating ice cream.

At this point, YF has the magazine open. He turns a page and gives a mildly shocked reaction. He holds the magazine up close for a moment, then brings it back down.

YF. Well, would you look at that?!

YS. What? That Timex watch? Is it the new 1964 model?

YF. Son, that is no Timex watch. It's a status symbol. It screams to the world that whoever is wearing it has succeeded in life.

YM continues to hang clothes. She swats frantically but quietly. She swats at something, then runs around the laundry basket, taking silly high knee little steps, then resumes hanging clothes.

YS. A Timex does all that?

YF. That is no Timex, son. That is a Rolex President. It cost almost $70,000.

YS. What does it do that the Timex doesn't?

YF. Don't you listen? It is a status symbol, a piece of art that you wear and show off.

YS. I'd rather have a home and a new car.

YF. We have a nice apartment, and what's wrong with our car?

YS. Yes, the apartment is nice, but wouldn't you rather have your own home? And the car is fine when it runs… (*Pauses.*) and stops. Father, have you seen my magic marker?

YF. Sorry son, I haven't but I'll help you look later.

YS. Groovy. Father, what is Mother doing?

YF. She's eating ice cream; what do you think she's doing?

YS. Laundry?

YF. Yes, she is doing woman's work.

YS. But aren't we all on vacation? Shouldn't you help her?

YF. No, like I said, it's women's work. A man shouldn't be seen doing women's work.

YS. But we are all alone at camp. Who will see you?

YF. You're missing the point. It's not dignified for a man to do laundry. Say, are you a sissy boy?

YS. What is a sissy boy?

YF. A boy who likes other boys more than he likes girls.

YS. Well, guys are swell, but someday I'll marry a girl like mother. Just not so old.

YF. Old? We're both in our mid-thirties!

YS. Yes. Like I said, you both have one foot in the grave. I don't want to marry someone so ancient.

YF. Ancient?! Get out of here and let me relax.

YS. OK, bye.

YS jumps off the chair, skips twice around the two chairs, then skips towards mother. He runs into a sheet on the laundry line. He is facing mother. Mother grabs the son, wrapping him momentarily in the sheet and laughs.

YM. You silly boy, what are you doing?

YS. Mother, father asked if I'm a sissy boy.

YM. Oh, for heaven's sake, no. Not that it'd matter to me. You may be a momma's boy.

YS. What is that?

YF continues to stare at the magazine at times, bringing it momentarily closer to his face.

YM. It's when a son loves his mother more than he loves himself.

YS. Oh, then I am a momma's boy!

YM. Yes, you are. Now why don't you go put on your new swimsuit and go for a swim?

YS. Ok, but I'll be back to help with the laundry.

YF. Wife, please come here. I want to show you something.

YM. OK dear, I'll be right there.

YM swats at something then walks over to father and stands behind him.

YM. What would you like to show me?

YF. This. Isn’t it beautiful?

YM. It seems a bit gaudy to me. What’s wrong with your Timex?

YF. I swear, you and our son are birds of a feather! If I had gotten that promotion, I could save up for this. It shows that a man is successful. That he’s made it.

YM. I'd rather make a bed in our own home.

YF. Our apartment is fine. Maybe you could take on a part-time job and help me save for this.

YM. Oh, for heaven's sake. That would cut into my volunteer time. And between that and taking care of my two lovelies, I truly have little time to myself as it is. OH! What is that, dear?

YF. What?

YM. That stain on your new shirt!

Father looks down and the pen has leaked. (This can be done by using a small needleless syringe, like a pharmacy dosing syringe. When he put it in his pocket he could push some liquid out.) YF looks at his shirt.

YF. Oh dear. I found our son's missing magic marker on the lawn, and I put it in my shirt pocket.

YM. Oh, for heaven's sake!

YF. Sweetie pie?

YM. Yes husband?

YF. I forgot something in town, I'll be quick and be back well before supper.

YM. Ok dear, but could you pick me up more laundry detergent and two cans of Dinty More stew?

YF. Sure, peaches.

YM. Oh, and two cans of sliced peaches in heavy syrup!

YF. You got it honeybun.

YM. (*Puts a forefinger to her lips.*)

Hmm, honeybuns, nah.

Lights over chairs dim out while lights over pawn shop turn on. Pawn Shop Owner (PS) is combing his hair in front of a wall mirror, stops, then pretends he is Maestro and uses comb as baton. Bell over door rings; he suddenly stops, goes to short leg of L shaped counter, and starts cleaning. On the counter is a clear spray bottle, filled ¾ with dark blue water. A mega sized roll of paper towels sits beside it. At the end of the short section of the cabinet is a tall-back wooden chair. A Halloween style skeleton sits in it. It is wearing a Santa Claus hat, and its hands are in its lap. The right hand is folded. (Audience can't see the detail, and the middle finger is extended. It is attached with fishing line to a pole that someone off stage can control.) The skeleton is wearing a brassiere and panties.

YF. Hello, sir.

PS. Hello, sir. May I help you find something?

YF. Do you have any men's watches?

PS. Yes, I have several. Anything in particular?

YF. Yes, I'm looking for a Rolex.

PS. Oh dear, it went out the door an hour ago. Check on Saturday. That is when I re-do the men's watch section.

YF. Okey Dokey, I'll see you on Saturday.

As YF prepares to exit stage left, he notices the skeleton.

YF. Good grief, what is that?

PS. Oh, that's Sally. She isn't much to look at but she sure is loyal!

YF. Whatever you say.

He shakes his head as he exits. Just as he is out of sight, the right arm of Sally raises, giving YF the finger.

PS. Sally, quit that! He may be a customer someday, though I doubt it.

Lights remain on the shop as YF positions himself in front of YM. YF is carrying a grocery bag. PS goes back to mirror and plays maestro again. Lights over the shop go out, spot lights on the chairs turn back on as do lights over YM. YS is busy fussing with the hung clothes.

YF. Honey, I got your groceries. (*He sets them on top of the laundry basket.*)

YM. Did the package with my award from Volunteer Services arrive?

YF. I'm not sure. I did my errand, got your supplies, and hurried back.

YF returns to his chair and opens the magazine. YS says 'Bye' to YM, then skips around the two chairs. YF, who had the magazine close to his face, lowers the magazine down enough to look at his son. As YS goes to exit stage right, first he takes his hat off and throws it into the audience like a frisbee, then as he leaves, he kicks the beach ball into the audience. As he leaves, he giggles.

YS. MacMillan!

YF. (*To himself.*) Where does he get those clothes?

Curtains close. With curtain closed, YS reappears from stage right. He slowly skips across the stage singing Mommas boy repeatedly.

He is wearing an old-fashioned men's swimsuit that covers most of his torso. He has a vivid beach towel draped around his neck. As he is about to exit, he turns and

faces the audience, takes the towel off, balls it up, and throws it into the audience while shouting:

YS. I'm a momma's boy!

He then exits and continues singing for two refrains.

YS. (CONT'D) I'm a momma's boy.

BLACKOUT.

Scammed

SETTING: *Teenage Son (TS) sits in an old, overstuffed chair toward middle of stage right. He has his right leg overhanging the arm of the chair. An old floor lamp is turned on illuminating the chair. A bookcase (4x4) is on the stage right of chair. It is messy, packed with books and magazines. Theme song from the odd movie 'Brazil' is softly playing.*

In front and off center towards stage left is an old kitchen table. The table can be a folding table but should have a red and white checkered tablecloth that overhangs by two feet. A teapot sits near an edge. There are four old chairs. The table sits toward the middle of stage left. Two of the chairs face the audience. Older Father (OF) sits at table facing the audience.

OF. Son, come into the kitchen and take a break from your studies and take a look at this and learn something important. Something you won't learn in college.

TS. OK, father. Something you picked up while on a business trip to New York city. Is it more important than studying for my medical entrance exam?

YF. Yes, this is something you won't learn in medical school.

YM is crossing the stage with a full laundry basket, she looks at her son.

YM. A doctor! My son is going to be a doctor!

TS. Mom, that's four years away. If it weren't for you taking me on your volunteer trips to the hospital, I never would have accelerated my studies. I'm just eighteen with a degree in psychology!

YM. What do you plan to specialize in?

TS. Heart surgery. I plan to work at Inner City hospital. Dr. Swahili already got me a part-time job there. Once I have my license, I'll work three days a week there. Then I plan on opening a free children's clinic that'll be open three days a week. I just don't know what to call it.

YM. How about Sonny's Children's Clinic?

TS. Nah, I want to name it after you and, while I adore your first name,

Philomena's Children's Clinic doesn't seem right.

YM. How about Mother's Children Clinic?

TS. Nah, I'll just get mothers. I want to use my medical and psychology degree to help kids. I got it! Momma's Boy Children's Clinic.

YM. Oh honey, I'm so proud of you. When you're ready, I have a surprise for you. A private account just for such a purpose.

TS. You're the best!

YF. Son, I don't have all day.

Son sits a heavy book down on the floor, gets up and takes a seat next to father.

TS. Wow, don't tell me you bought that watch you've been obsessed over since the time we went to camp.

OF. I don't obsess; it's just something I desire. To say I bought it might be a misnomer. You might say I stole it.

TS. Father!

OF. Relax, I'm exaggerating. See, there was this guy I met on a sidewalk. He was poorly dressed and had a bit of body odor. He said he was selling off some of his deceased father's belongings. He showed me this watch and said his father wore it all his life, up to a couple of years ago. The watch had stopped running as it needed a deep cleaning that his father couldn't afford. He said he didn't know much about watches, but I was told this was worth a lot of money. He was asking for a thousand dollars. If it was working it might be worth five hundred dollars, but like it is, one hundred. He said he understood, and said how about two hundred? I said "deal." There just happened to be one of those automatic banking machines there, so I withdrew two hundred dollars. Not bad for your old man, eh?

TS. Cool, let me see it.

OF. Ok, but be careful, this might be worth thousands once it's cleaned.

TS takes watch and examines it closely. He sets watch down, goes to bookcase and takes magnifier glass off the top shelf and returns to kitchen table and re-examines the watch.

TS. Father, oh father!

OF. What? Is it engraved?

TS. Not exactly.

OF. Well, what is it?

TS. Father, I hate to tell you this…

OF. Spit it out son, what is it?

TS. Father, you were scammed. Welcome to big city life.

OF. What is it? What do you mean, scammed?

TS. This isn't a Rolex.

OF. Just how do you know? It says Rolex right on the face.

TS. You mean right next to Roman number two which is missing half of it?

OF. Gimme that before you break it. (*Son hands father the watch.*) Well, if it isn't a Rolex, what is it?

TS. Do you really want to know?

OF. Quit playing games, what is it?

TS. It's a Timex.

OF. NO!

Mother is crossing back holding an empty laundry basket in one hand.

YM. Oh, for heaven's sake.

Mother quickly exits, goggling to herself.

TS. Yes, it says so in tiny letters on the back.

YM gives a loud 'Ha' from out of sight.

OF. I don't believe you; I'll take it to the pawn shop and show you!

Father gets up to head stage right. Lights over kitchen scene dim while lights over pawn shop turn on. The spray bottle of blue liquid is now half full. (It would be easiest to have the three bottles prepared so liquid doesn't need to be emptied.) The paper towel roll is now much thinner. PS is center stage. In his right hand he holds an arm from a mannequin, and he sings loudly and poorly while acting as a maestro with the arm. Bell over the door drops and he rushes behind the counter. The bottle is ¼ full, and few paper towels remain.

PS. Well if it isn't the big city businessman! Back so soon?

PS removes his glasses and lets them hang on a chain around his neck.

OF. Yes, thankfully it was a quick trip. I don't know how people live there, shoulder to shoulder!

A bell, like that attached to a door, rings.

PS. Excuse me for a moment.

A woman in casual clothes enters from the end of the shop's counter.

MW. Toodle loo!

PS. That was fast, I haven't even put your wedding rings on display!

MW. Oh, don't I know it? I just love that cranky ole fool.

PS reaches for a small manilla envelope. The envelope should look a little bulky. He hands it to MW as she approaches him. MW slaps down a pile of money, all in bills. PS picks up a couple of the bills.

PS. Here, take this back. You're such a regular customer I won't charge you a handling fee this time. Heck, you're here so much I should offer you a job!

MW. Wouldn't that be something? Careful, don't say something you might regret later!

MW exits stage left and gives out a loud laugh "Ha." PS looks back at OF. As she leaves, she gives Sally a light pat on the head. Sally has a large cigar in her mouth. As MW leaves, Sally, with a full hand, waves goodbye.

PS. Good girl, Sally!

OF. Wow, she's a piece of work!

PS. Oh, she marches to the beat of her own drummer all right, but she's a sweetheart.

OF. Guess the mental wards are all filled up.

PS. Don't be like that, you don't know her. But New York City, yeah, I know what you mean, shoulder to shoulder. I was there twenty years ago. Once is enough for me! Say, what do you have there?

OF. You tell me.

OF hands PS the watch and takes a step back. PS takes watch then puts his glasses on. He turns on a round lighted magnifier glass sitting on the counter. He examines the watch.

PS. Where did you get this?

OF. (*In a huff.*) Never mind, just tell me what it is and how much it's worth.

PS. It's a cheap Rolex knockoff, not even well done. It's an old Timex, and it's worthless.

OF. Damn, he was right. I promise not to tell anyone, but I got scammed in the big city. Thought I was smarter than that.

PS. Can I offer a word of advice?

OF. Of course, I welcome it.

PS. Don't get hung up on material goods, they can be the death of you and destroy your family.

OF. No worries there. I just think that Rolex is beautiful.

PS. Your family is beautiful, a watch is just a watch.

PS removes his glasses and puts watch on the counter. Father steps up and retrieves the watch.

OF. I hear you; I learned that lesson in the war.

PS. Hey don’t feel bad. Your secret is safe with me. We all get scammed occasionally. Look you’ve been coming in here, for what, damn near every Saturday for nearly a decade now, looking for a deal on a Rolex. You thought you found it and your emotions got the best of you. Say, how much did it set you back?

OF. Two hundred. That was supposed to buy my wife an anniversary gift.

PS. Ouch.

CURTAIN CLOSES.

Betrayal

SETTING: *A tall counter positioned on the stage left. It has not lit up yet. A sign overhead reads receptionist for Dr. Swahili. The song 'Cry Me A River' is playing softly throughout this scene.*

AT RISE: *The scene opens with PS. Now balding, he is wearing his glasses on the tip of his nose, singing along with a song, but he is facing the audience in front of his counter.*

And he is dancing with Sally. Her Dolly Parton style wig stays on. He waltzes around the stage, dipping Sally a couple of times. At one point he hits his glasses from his face. Bell over rear door, out of sight, rings. OF enters. PS stops dancing and quickly puts Sally back in her chair. He rushes to be behind the counter and starts cleaning the countertop. The spray bottle is empty and only the inner cardboard tube for paper towels remains.

OF. Were you just…

PS. …cleaning the countertop, yes, I was. Is it Saturday already?

OF. Why, I believe it is.

PS. Well, it's a good thing you stopped in, because I have a surprise for you!

OF. Spill the beans, spill the beans!

PS. I don't think you know her, but Mrs. MacMillan stopped in this morning.

OF. No, the name doesn't sound familiar. What did she want?

PS. Her husband, Clay 'Beachball' MacMillan died recently. She doesn't need money as he earned millions off his patent on a cheaper way to make beach balls. She brought in something special. Here, look. (*Bell over door rings.*)

MW. Toodle loo!

The same exchange as before, this time there is no need for PS to return money. MW enters and leaves quickly, without further talking, except as she leaves. OF is watching her and seems mesmerized.

MW. Ool eldoot.

OF looks at PS and OF raises both elbows up as if to say 'WTF.'

PS. Oh, that's her new way of saying goodbye. It's 'toodle loo' backwards.

OF. I think it translates to "I'm nuts."

PS. Let her be, I like her. She brightens my day.

OF shakes his head while PS reaches underneath and puts a large watch on the counter.

PS. The best thing is the banks aren't open yet and she needed some quick cash, so I opened my safe.

OF. Is that what I think it is?

PS. Yes, the one and only Rolex, President model. Clay thought they were gaudy and preferred his Timex!

He wore it for less than a year. It's been in a case since the 1960's!

OF. Oh my, it's beautiful. But how much is it?

PS. The icing on the cake is she needed twenty-two thousand exactly. I could retire with this, but as you've been coming in since I opened my shop – though you haven't bought a thing – I'll let you have it for what I have in it. I know it's more than you can afford, but I'd be willing to do a lay-away plan.

OF. No way!

PS. Way.

OF. Let me write you a check right now!

PS. Is the check rubber?

OF. Ha ha! No, I inherited some money. Let me go get the checkbook.

OF walks out stage left. PS goes and adjusts the skeleton. Bell over door rings and OF enters from rear.

PS. Would you like it bagged, or would you prefer to wear it now?

OF. Oh, it's going on my wrist right now and not coming off!

OF exits (either side is fine), lights go out. Talking from behind the receptionist counter starts. Though the audience can't see her, MW is in an old school nurse's uniform to prepare her for the next scene. There is slightly muffled talk between a man (son can do this, disguise voice) and a woman.

MAN. I don't know what is happening. Where is the spotlight?

WOMAN. Amos must have fallen asleep again. Go wake him up.

MAN. (*Screams.*) AMOS!

WOMAN. Shh, not like that!

From the rear of the audience (the person running the lights can do this):

LIGHTS PERSON. (O.S.) Sorry.

WOMAN. What on earth are you doing?

LIGHTS PERSON. (O.S.) I got hooked looking at this ad for a watch.

WOMAN. Let me guess, a Rolex?

LIGHTS PERSON. (O.S.) Oh, for heavens no, much too gaudy. This is a slick new Timex! I'm going to Watches R Us as soon as I'm done here.

From rear of stage, OM shouts.

OM. (O.S.) Oh, for heaven's sake!

MW. Done here? Amos, this might be your last show!

Spotlight turns on but is aimed down at audience. The light sweeps frantically over the audience, walls, and stage, then comes to rest on receptionist desk. OF is there. MW is standing behind the counter.

OF. I'll have it next month.

MW. You know I can't do that. Against the rules I've already let you slide for six months. Do you work for free?

OF. Of course not but have a heart. I'd do it for you.

MW. You said the same thing last month. And we don't work for free either. For your wife to see the oncologist, we need the whole amount to get you current, twenty-two thousand dollars.

OF. OK, wife has the checkbook. I'll be back in a few minutes.

MW. Don't be too long, you're already late as it is. Say, nice watch. I bet one of our oncologists would pay you for what you owe for that watch. It's a Rolex, right?

OF extends his arm for MW to get a better look. OF turns the watch on his wrist (audience only sees OF stretching his arm over the counter) and the band breaks, causing the watch to fall off.

OF. Damn, the band broke!

MW. Don't fret; this happened the other day to Dr. Swahili's Rolex. I can do a temporary fix in a jiffy. There you go. Sure you don't want to sell it?

OF. No way, but thanks, she's a beauty. I met a guy way up north who is a certified Rolex repair man. I'll make an appointment with him. These witch Doctors make too much as it is. I'll be right back.

OF walks to center stage. Spotlight is on OM sitting in a folding chair center front stage, she is clutching an old purse. Set back enough for following to occur. Her head is lowered, she is wearing a black ratty wig.

OF. Good news, wife.

OM. Oh. What is that?

OF. Doc says latest blood work says you're doing fine, and you can skip this month. Let's get out of here before they change their mind.

OM. Are you sure? I certainly don't feel better. My stomach feels like I swallowed a beachball! Say, that gives me time to go to the children's ward. Just let me get my rat, er, wig. I'll meet you in the parking garage.

OF. Oh sugar, not today, I have errands to run. Tell you what, we'll go shopping for a new rat, and next month I'll bring you an hour early so you can see the kids, OK? First let's go home and have a cup of tea. This place gives me the heebie geebies.

OM. Oh you're always thinking of me. Dear, is that a new watch? (*She stands up while adjusting her wig.*)

OF. Oh, this old thing? I picked it up at the pawn shop this morning.

OM. You bought something there? Oh, for heaven's sake, I suppose after all these years it was bound to happen. I hope it didn't cost too much. Say, have you seen my private checkbook?

OF. Sorry dear, I didn't know we had more than one. The watch was a steal.

OM. Um hmm, I've heard that before. Please keep an eye for my checkbook, it's money I tuck away in case of an emergency.

MW enters as nurse on stage right. OM, as she stands up, is adjusting her wig, just as MW nears OM. OM knocks wig onto floor. OF picks it up high and shakes it near MW's face. MW screams.

MW. Ahh! Oh dear, I thought it was a rat!

OF. No, just my wife's wig.

OF shakes the wig in face of MW, who snatches wig, and as she passes receptionist desk, she tosses it over. Multiple screams.

MW. Get that woman a real wig!

MW exits stage right as light fades out.

CURTAIN CLOSES.

<u>The Office</u>

SETTING: *A large desk, with no drawers, sits on center stage. A high back chair is behind it. A brass lamp with a green shade is on the desk. OF sits in the chair. He is staring at something on the desk and is smiling. Adult Son (AS) enters stage right, he walks toward desk, stands off center so Adult Father (AF) can be seen. "The*

Chain" by Fleetwood Mac plays softly.

AS. Oh, the irony.

AF. Son, whatever do you mean?

AS. The only way you could afford all of this is with mother's insurance money.

AF. Not true, I'm a highly successful business man. I have been all my life.

AS. You live in an alternate universe. What are you looking at? Oh, the watch is more important than your grandson's first piano recital? Don't worry, I will cover for you. I told him you're sick. I just left out the word "mentally."

OF. Oh son, don't be like that. You know I'm busy.

AS. You're retired, except for staring at the watch.

OF. I promise to make it up to him.

AS. It's about the watch, isn't it? Hasn't it always been about the watch? You have it there, splayed out with its alligator bands, just like new, except for that impression across that one particular hole. So well preserved, mocking me. When hasn't it been about the watch? Precious thing. More important than anything, anyone else. The watch. Now here, of all places, sitting on that dark golden oak table, the color of which can only be achieved though age, sits the watch. Timeless. Ticking. Tormenting. The audacity of having it there, sitting in the fading sun. Glistening. You know I can't keep my eyes off it, the watch. When will it be over? Ever? How can anything physical have so much meaning? Here, I pace around this vast, hollow, damp room, and there it is. Why? Why place it there? Why isn't it where I've seen a picture of it all my life? Why have it in this room, on this table, today? Of all things in my life, that I'll remember the most is the watch. Watching the watch. Being told about the watch. Story after story about the watch. I want to smash it. Is that why it is here? A test? A test of my resolve against the watch? You know it represents so much more than a timepiece. The watch. It is all your life lessons distilled into a single mechanical possession. A history book of sorts. Here, in this timeless room, the watch. I will not give you what you seek. I will not release my own traits. You can keep it. The watch.

AS starts to leave, turns back, picks up the watch, places it on the floor and smashes his heel into it. OF gasps as he picks it up and places it back on the desk.

AS. There, now it's as broken as I am.

CURTAIN CLOSES.

Cemetery Part I

SETTING: *Single headstone that reads 'Mother' on stage left. OF enters from stage right, he is limply holding flowers in his left hand, He*

shuffles toward the grave. He gently places the flowers in front of the headstone. Sobbing, he leans over and rest his crossed forearms and head on top of the headstone.

OF. Honey, I'm so sorry, please forgive me.

Sound of a mourning dove momentarily over rides the music. OF places right hand over his heart and slowly lays down across Mother's grave.

CLAY HURTUBISE

CURTAIN CLOSES.

Cemetery Part II

SETTING: *Two tombstones face each other, separated by several feet. A third tombstone is behind them. AS enters from stage left. He is dressed in a suit with a hat and places flowers at one of the opposing graves – the one towards stage left. He picks up older flowers and tosses them off stage. When he addresses mother, he looks at headstone on his stage left side, father is on stage right side.*

The song 'Hurt,' Johnny Cash version, is playing softly. AS is looking at mother's headstone. On stage right front are two old style galvanized buckets. A long handle spade shovel sits on auditorium floor and rests against the stage.

AS. Sorry mother. I just couldn't have him buried with you. Not after what he did. (*AS turns slowly to look at father's headstone.*) Father, I suppose you should know this. Dr. Swahili's office called mother after the first missed appointment, and they told mother everything. After the second missed appointment, when you were out of town having the watch cleaned, they said they would have to wait six weeks and restart the latest round of chemotherapy. Of course, she would never get that as she died four weeks later.

MW enters from stage left. She is dressed all in black with a thin black veil over her face. She has on a small black hat that the veil is attached to. She is sobbing uncontrollably.

MW. Oh Henry, Oh Henry.

She repeats this as she walks past AS and goes towards the third headstone. She carelessly tosses the flowers at the grave, which is overflowing with flowers. At this point, PS crosses at front of stage from stage right. PS is holding

Sally, so Sally is closest to audience (her left leg is tied to PS's right leg), a metal bucket is on the foot closest to audience, and she is wearing the same hat and veil as MW. MW looks up. When she is about one-third across the stage, MW looks up and turns towards Sally.

MW. AHHHH!

AS. Don't worry ma'am, he's just walking Sally. She is his deceased wife. Evidently, she was wearing her prized pearl necklace which got caught in the machinery and pulled her over the railing into a vat of acid. That's all that's left of her. He wired the bones together. (*Looking over at her.*) Ma'am, I'm sorry about your loss. If I'm not rude, is your husband buried there?

MW turns to look at AS, then walks toward him. She stops sobbing and puts the veil over her hat and talks in a normal voice. PS and Sally exit stage left.

MW. My husband? Oh, for heaven's sake, no. He's parked over there. (*She points to rear of audience.*) This is the grave of our dog, Oh Henry,' like the candy bar. See, he was a chocolate lab, and he reminded my husband of the candy bar, Oh Henry. He thinks I loved him as much as he did. He didn't have to take care of that fur shedding, stinky mutt like I did. I thought he'd never die. Oh, what a relief it is!

AS. Then why all the drama?

MW. Excuse me, I should be wiping away tears at this point. (*She pulls out a handkerchief, dabs her eyes then blows her nose.*) We couldn't have kids. Though we tried. Lord almighty, we tried. He treated that mutt like his only child. This is an act that I hope I can quit soon. He can't bear to visit the grave; he doesn't even park close.

But believe me, he is watching my every move.

AS. Well I can play along. Here, give me a hug.

MW. Oh, you're a dear. He'll love this.

AS. All in a day's work.

MW. One other thing. My sister was married to the balloon man, and she wants me to find good homes for his watch collection. You take this and do with it as you please. (*She reaches into her pocket and pulls out a jewelry* *box. She hands it too AS.*) Do you have children?

AS. I do. Two. A boy and a girl.

MW. Then it's important you don't break the seal. A sealed one can be worth twice that of an unsealed one. Here, take this key and card; I have a safety deposit box pre-paid for ten years. See this gentleman, he is expecting someone. By the time your kids are ready for college, this should pay their way.

AS. I don't know what to say. A thank you doesn't seem sufficient.

MW. I agree, you owe me another hug. It's time for me to return to my grieving husband.

MW turns to exit stage left. Just before she leaves, AS calls after her.

AS. Ma'am?

MW. Yes dear?

AS. If you get another dog, could you do me a favor?

MW. And what would that be?

AS. Name him Snickers.

MW. Oh, for heaven's sake, that is precious! I will!

MW exits while both are laughing.

Just after she exits, we hear from off stage:

MW. (O.S.) Snickers! Ha, I love it.

AS is quiet for a moment as he stands between the two graves.

AS. Father, did you catch all that? I'll be back next week.

AS exits stage left. It is quiet for a moment. The headstones are lit up by the spotlight. OM's voice will be from stage left, while OF's voice will be from stage right.

OF. Wife, I'm so sorry, can you ever forgive me?

OM. Oh, for heaven's sake, I forgave you when I was alive.

OF. Seriously? Why didn't you tell me what the doctor's office called?

OM. I knew how much that silly watch meant to you. Do you think I didn't know what was happening? I must say, I was surprised when you missed the second appointment.

OF. Yes, I haven't forgiven myself for that selfish act.

OM. Husband, please let it go. I'll tell you something.

OF. Oh, what's that?

OM. See, it was almost a relief to me when the chemo got cancelled.

Undergoing that, throwing up several times a day, always terribly weak, I was the walking dead.

OF. I'm sorry I didn't do more for you.

OM. Not much you could have done. I did my homework, people with my cancer only live a few more months on average than those without treatment. Going off chemo gave me two decent months while with chemo I would have felt miserable every day.

I'm happy with how things worked out.

OF. So being with me and my obsession wasn't a burden?

OM. I always loved you. If I were to use one word to describe living with you, that word would be…

OF. Go on, say it!

OM. Challenge. (*She giggles*.)

OF. Then could you do me a huge favor?

OM. Sure husband, what is it?

OF. Get through to son and ask him to have our graves side by side.

OM. Consider it done.

AS reemerges and walks toward the far side of the headstones so he is facing the audience.

AS. Mother, father, I've been thinking.

OF. Uh oh, he's going to have me cremated and sprinkle my ashes over the Timex factory!

OM. Oh, for heaven's sake! He will not. Maybe over the beachball factory! (*OM laughs*.)

AS. I've been thinking, mother is such a forgiving soul, I shouldn't keep you two separated. On my way out, I'll talk to the manager here and have you share a double plot.

AS exits stage left.

OF. Wow wife, that was fast!

OM. Well, he is a momma's boy!

Curtain closes. AS enter from stage right. He is well dressed and wearing a hat as he slowly walks to center stage, takes off his hat, and throws it into the audience and shouts.

AS. I'm still a mommas' boy!

AS exits stage left singing 'I'm still a momma's boy.' He repeats this loudly twice once off stage.

BLACKOUT.

THE END

BOWS

The curtain opens and cast bow. PS is holding Sally by his side. When they bow, Sally's wig falls off. The curtain closes momentarily, then reopens, house lights come on. Cast members file through auditorium, taking different routes. They, along with spotlight operator, position themselves at the exits and thank the audience.

Other books by Clay Hurtubise, R. Ph.

Drug Trip: A memoir While a student at the school of pharmacy at the University of Wyoming, the school sponsored a 'drug trip' to the mid-west to visit pharmaceutical companies. Lacking the funds to go on the trip, he jumped on his Yamaha 650 and headed for the Pacific coast.

On the first day he drives through a snow squall, is in a traumatic accident, and someone tries to kill him. Waking up the next morning he continues his journey thinking It must get better, but does it?

Shaman: Devil's Deal chronicles the life of a young shaman who must learn his powers quickly, as an evil force has invaded his neighborhood. Learning the meaning of family, he finds himself, and his new family, stronger than he ever imagined.

CAW: An innovative bilingual book.

English is on one side, while the same content is on the opposite page in another language. It is meant to strengthen the readers' reading skills. The story is of an evil farmer who takes over an organic farm in Maine, then proceeds to use chemicals and poisons. This results in the death of a congress of Ravens, all except for one; CAW. He must venture out into the world where he will be scorned and learn life lessons. In the end, due to his deformity, he saves the day.

Feathers: The sequel to CAW. In Feathers, an unlikely group of animals band together. They face multiple threats and defeat them. Along the way a misguided little boy is wounded and lost. Saved by the animals, the boy is transformed.

If Only (due out 2025): A collection of true short stories. Who hasn’t had an If Only moment? If only I used the numbers I intended for the lottery, if only I had introduced myself to the hottie at the bar, if only I didn't have that last 'one for the road.' Readers will be able to submit their own If Only story for publication, much like they can do for Ghost Stories, readers edition. See either book for details.

Made in the USA
Columbia, SC
01 March 2025

b13ce525-40e5-4424-ba7f-526d65dc7247R01